PRESIDENTS OF THE U.S.A.

CALVIN COOLIDGE

OUR THIRTIETH PRESIDENT

by Melissa Maupin

THE CHILD'S WORLD®

PUBLISHED IN THE UNITED STATES OF AMERICA

THE CHILD'S WORLD®
1980 Lookout Drive • Mankato, MN 56003-1705
800-599-READ • www.childsworld.com

ACKNOWLEDGMENTS
The Child's World®: Mary Berendes, Publishing Director

Creative Spark: Mary McGavic, Project Director; Melissa McDaniel, Editorial
Director; Deborah Goodsite, Photo Research

The Design Lab: Kathleen Petelinsek, Design; Gregory Lindholm, Page Production

Content Adviser: David R. Smith, Adjunct Assistant Professor of History,
University of Michigan–Ann Arbor

PHOTOS
Cover and page 3: White House Historical Association (White House Collection)
(detail); White House Historical Association (White House Collection)

Interior: Alamy: 24 (Folio Inc.); The Art Archive: 20, 29 (Culver Pictures);
Associated Press Images: 5, 8, 18, 35; Corbis: 10, 34 (Corbis), 19, 21, 22, 26,
28 and 39, 37 (Bettmann), 25 (Oscar White); The Calvin Coolidge Presidential
Library and Museum at Forbes Library, Northampton, Massachusetts: 4 and 38,
6, 7, 13, 16, 32 and 39; Getty Images: 30 (Hulton Archive); The Image Works: 14
(Scherl/SV-Bilderdienst), 27 (Mary Evans Picture Library); iStockphoto: 44 (Tim
Fan); Library of Congress: 11, 12; U.S. Air Force photo: 45.

LIBRARY OF CONGRESS CATALOGING-IN-PUBLICATION DATA
Maupin, Melissa, 1958–
  Calvin Coolidge / by Melissa Maupin.
      p. cm.— (Presidents of the U.S.A.)
  Includes bibliographical references and index.
  ISBN 978-1-60253-058-4 (library bound : alk. paper)
  1. Coolidge, Calvin, 1872–1933—Juvenile literature.
  2. Presidents—United States—Biography—Juvenile literature. I. Title.
  E792.M379 2008
  973.91'5'092—dc21

  [B]
                                      2007042600

President Calvin Coolidge in a portrait painted in 1932

TABLE OF CONTENTS

CHAPTER ONE

SILENT CAL

Calvin Coolidge was born on July 4, 1872, in a cottage in Plymouth Notch, Vermont. His mother, Victoria, was frail and frequently sick. She suffered from what at the time was called "consumption." Today we call this disease tuberculosis. Calvin and his younger sister, Abigail, learned to be quiet and well behaved so their mother could rest. This was not a problem for Calvin because he was naturally shy and quiet. Many years later, when Calvin Coolidge served as the 30th president of the United States, he was known as Silent Cal.

*Calvin Coolidge
at age three*

Calvin Coolidge's father, John, farmed the green rolling countryside of Vermont that Calvin would grow to love. John Coolidge also owned the town's general store. He served as tax collector and justice of the peace. And he was elected to the Vermont legislature, the part of the government that makes the state's laws.

Calvin Coolidge (left) and his father, John, on their farm in Vermont. Both Coolidges loved the Vermont countryside.

Victoria Coolidge began educating Calvin at a young age. She gave him blocks with letters of the alphabet and Roman numerals printed on them. "As I played with them and asked my mother what they were," he later wrote, "I came to know them all when I was three years old." He started school in 1877 when he was five years old. He was the youngest child in a one-room schoolhouse. He shared the class with 23 other children of all ages.

Calvin's mother,
Victoria, died when he
was just 12 years old.
He carried a picture
of her with him for
the rest of his life.

Young Calvin was smaller than other children his age. He had clear, blue eyes and red hair that gradually changed to dark blond. Because he was small, he didn't feel comfortable playing sports. He enjoyed horseback riding and fishing, however. He also helped his father on the farm, picking apples and collecting sap to make maple syrup.

For the most part, Calvin's childhood was peaceful and happy. But then, when he was 12 years old, his mother suffered a horrible accident. She fell from a runaway horse and was severely injured. Already weak, Victoria Coolidge died soon after the accident. Years later, Calvin Coolidge looked back on her death, saying, "The greatest grief that can come to a boy came to me. Life was never the same again."

Calvin attended high school at the Black River Academy in the town of Ludlow, 12 miles away from his home. He lived at the academy and sometimes walked home on weekends to visit his family. In the summers, he would go home and help his father run the farm. Calvin was a good student. He was well-liked by his classmates for his dry sense of humor.

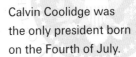

Calvin Coolidge was the only president born on the Fourth of July.

In 1904, Coolidge took his first car ride with a neighbor. After the ride, he told his neighbor, "It's wonderful to ride in a horseless carriage, but it won't amount to much." He meant that he didn't think cars would become common.

Calvin Coolidge attended Black River Academy as a teenager. He graduated in 1890.

Calvin Coolidge became a top student at Amherst College. "You can't know too much," he once said, "but you can say too much."

Coolidge framed and hung the following poem on his living room wall:

*A wise old owl lived
     in an oak.
The more he saw,
     the less he spoke.
The less he spoke
     the more he heard.
Why can't we be
     like that old bird?*

During his senior year, Calvin Coolidge suffered another tragic loss. His sister, Abigail, became gravely ill with appendicitis. Calvin stayed at Abigail's bedside as she grew weaker and then died. The only way Calvin could deal with his grief was by studying even harder and preparing for college.

Right before Calvin's first year at Amherst College in Massachusetts, John Coolidge remarried. His new wife, Carrie, was a teacher. Calvin liked and respected Carrie very much.

Calvin struggled during his first two years at Amherst, but his grades improved in the final two years. He graduated with honors in 1895. Calvin decided to become a lawyer. After graduation, he began working as an assistant at a law firm in Northampton, Massachusetts. He also studied for the exams that he would have to pass to become a lawyer. Two years later, he earned his certificate to work as a lawyer and opened his own office.

As he worked to find clients, Coolidge also worked for the **Republican Party,** one of the country's two major **political parties.** His efforts paid off. Within a year, Coolidge was elected to a seat on the Northampton City Council. It was the first of many political positions that he would hold on his way to the White House. Over the next few years, Coolidge would be elected city attorney and clerk of courts for Hampshire County.

During this time, he lived in a simple boardinghouse. Next door to this house was a school for deaf children. A young teacher named Grace Goodhue worked at the school. One day when she was watering flowers outside, Goodhue caught a glimpse of Coolidge through his window. He was wearing long underwear and shaving. She laughed at the sight, and Coolidge turned to see her leaving. He found out her name and asked to be introduced to her.

Grace Goodhue was the opposite of Coolidge in many ways. She had a warm, friendly personality and rarely felt shy. She and Coolidge liked each other right

As a child, Coolidge was nicknamed "Red" because of his red hair.

Coolidge's name at birth was John Calvin Coolidge, just like his father. In college, he went by J. Calvin, and as a young adult, he dropped the John and went by Calvin.

Calvin's sister, Abigail, became a schoolteacher when she was only 13 years old.

Calvin Coolidge graduated *cum laude*, meaning "with honors," from Amherst College in 1895. His classmates chose him to give the Grove Oration at his graduation. This was a humorous speech given at every Amherst graduation.

away and married on October 4, 1905. She was the only woman he had ever dated. A year later, Coolidge was elected to the Massachusetts House of Representatives. He was reelected the next year but resigned after that **term.** By then, he and Grace had two sons, John and Calvin Jr.

Coolidge next began to **campaign** to become the mayor of Northampton. Despite his shyness, he made a big effort to meet voters. Sometimes he stopped people on the street and asked them to vote for him. People found him to be a simple, straightforward man, and he won the election.

Grace Coolidge was both stylish and active. She loved hiking and horseback riding.

THE OTHER SIDE OF SILENT CAL

Calvin Coolidge was famously quiet and shy, but he also
had another side. With people he knew well, he talked
easily. Friends even called him talkative. Coolidge was
well read and could discuss almost any subject.

Coolidge was not fond of speaking in public, yet
he gave more speeches than any other president. At
meetings with reporters, called press conferences,
Coolidge often gave short answers. Still, he held more
of these meetings than any other president.

When he met with reporters, he asked them not to
take notes, but he let them take his picture. In fact, Coolidge
seemed to enjoy posing for the camera. In the picture above,
Coolidge is being presented with a warbonnet during a
ceremony making him an honorary chief of the Lakota people.

Coolidge was also the first president to star in a film.
He let a director make a silent movie about him. Coolidge
wore a cowboy costume in one part of the film.

CHAPTER TWO

THE COOLIDGE LUCK

After serving two terms as mayor, Coolidge won a seat in the Massachusetts state senate. He served two terms and he decided to leave politics. But then he heard some interesting news. The president of the state senate, Levi Greenwood, was going to run for the job of lieutenant governor. A lieutenant governor is the person who is second in command of a state government. Rather than retire, Coolidge decided to run for the senate again with the hope of becoming the senate president the following term. But then Greenwood changed his mind. Instead of running for lieutenant governor, he ran for president of the senate again. But, as luck would have it, Greenwood lost the election. Coolidge campaigned to become president of the senate and was elected. Many called it "the Coolidge luck." Often during his career, Coolidge seemed to be in the right place at the right time.

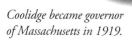

Coolidge became governor of Massachusetts in 1919.

Perhaps he was unusually lucky, but he also worked hard for his success and made good choices.

In 1915, Coolidge ran for lieutenant governor of Massachusetts. This meant that he had to campaign all around the state. At times, his shyness was still a problem. He often felt uncomfortable talking to strangers. "When I was a little fellow, I would go into a panic if I heard strange voices in the kitchen," he once said. "I felt I couldn't meet the people and shake hands with them . . . the hardest thing in the world was to have

Coolidge and his family pose for a picture at their home in Northampton, Massachusetts.

The sale of alcohol was outlawed in the United States during Coolidge's term as Massachusetts governor. Here, police dump out barrels of alcohol.

to go through the kitchen door and give them a greeting. I'm all right with old friends, but every time I meet a stranger, I've got to go through the old kitchen door—and it's not easy."

Coolidge won his bid for lieutenant governor and served three terms. He moved to Boston, but Grace Coolidge stayed in Northampton and raised the boys. After his third term as lieutenant governor, Coolidge ran for governor. One of his biggest supporters was Frank Stearns, a wealthy businessman. Stearns would continue to support Coolidge throughout his career. When the votes were counted, Coolidge won by almost 17,000.

As governor, he fought for better working conditions for all people. "We must humanize the industry, or the system will break down," he said. Coolidge approved a **bill** to limit the work week to 48 hours for women and children. He also pushed through a law to raise the amount of money employers paid workers if they were injured on the job. Coolidge tried to help **veterans** returning from World War I by solving a housing shortage so they could find places to live.

Coolidge signed into law a budget that kept the tax rates the same, while trimming four million dollars from expenses. Though he helped pass many bills, he also sometimes **vetoed,** or rejected, bills. As governor, he vetoed a bill that would allow the sale of beer or wine. He also turned down a bill that would raise the pay of legislators.

The most famous challenge that Coolidge faced as governor was the 1919 Boston police strike. This situation could have hurt Coolidge's career. Instead, the problem turned into another lucky boost for him. At that time, police officers performed difficult, dangerous work, just as they do today. But in Coolidge's time, they worked long hours for little pay. They also had to pay for their own uniforms. The police banded together to form a union, a group that fought for better pay and working conditions. The Boston police commissioner said that they could not be in a union and still perform

Coolidge had a flair for the written word. He wrote his own speeches and was the author of four books; *The Price of Freedom* (1919), *Have Faith in Massachusetts* (1919), *Foundations of the Republic* (1926), and *The Autobiography of Calvin Coolidge* (1929).

A law known as **Prohibition** went into effect January 16, 1920. It banned the manufacture and sale of alcoholic beverages in the United States. This law remained in effect throughout Coolidge's time as president. In 1933, the law was **repealed**.

Calvin Coolidge called in the National Guard to restore order during the Boston police strike.

their duties. The police responded angrily. Seventy-five percent of them decided to walk off the job.

With few police on duty, mobs roamed the streets of Boston, robbing and rioting. Citizens locked themselves in their houses and armed themselves with guns for protection. The next morning, the mayor of Boston, Andrew Peters, called in the state **militia** to take control of the city. Riots still continued that night. Two men were killed, and nine were wounded. The next day, Governor Coolidge called in the Massachusetts National Guard. They restored peace to Boston.

The police commissioner fired all the striking policemen. Coolidge supported this decision, even though he believed the policemen deserved higher pay and better working conditions. He explained his support of the commissioner by saying, "There is no right to strike against the public safety by anybody, anywhere, any time!"

Word spread around the country about the strike and Coolidge's bold words. Many people admired how he had handled the situation. Even President Woodrow Wilson sent a note of congratulations to Coolidge. The police strike made him popular. He easily won reelection as governor.

In 1920, members of the Republican Party held their national convention, where they would choose their next **candidate** for president of the United States. Coolidge's old friend Frank Stearns supported Coolidge as a candidate, but other convention **delegates** did not. In fact, no candidate won enough votes to win the **nomination.** Finally, several powerful senators held a secret meeting. They decided they wanted Senator Warren G. Harding of Ohio to be their candidate.

When the delegates met again the next day, the group of senators managed to push through Harding's name as the Republican candidate. Coolidge's luck came into play once again. The same group of senators

When Coolidge won the vice presidential nomination, delegates at the convention commented on his luck. One man said he wouldn't take the presidency for a million dollars with Coolidge as vice president. When asked why, he answered jokingly, "Because I would die in a little while." Oddly enough, this is exactly what happened. In 1923, President Warren Harding died, and Vice President Calvin Coolidge became president.

Attractive and well-educated, first lady Grace Coolidge was one of the most popular White House hostesses. In 1931, she was voted one of America's 12 greatest living women.

17

Once, Calvin Coolidge came home from Boston with a bag full of laundry. When Grace Coolidge opened it, there were 52 pairs of socks inside, each full of holes. Grace set to work mending them but later asked if he married her just to have someone to sew his socks. "No," he said seriously. "But I find it mighty handy."

President Coolidge loved the outdoors. He often fished during the summer. On a vacation in Wisconsin, Coolidge was asked how many fish he thought there were in the river. "About 45,000," he answered. "I haven't caught them all yet, but I've intimidated them."

Fishing was one of Calvin Coolidge's favorite activities.

tried to nominate Irvine L. Lenroot as the vice presidential candidate. This upset many delegates, who felt that the senators were forcing their own decisions onto the rest of the delegates. A delegate from Oregon stood up in protest and nominated Coolidge. Soon, others stood and shouted his name: "Coolidge! Coolidge! Coolidge!" In the end, he won a surprising victory and became the Republican vice presidential candidate.

SLEEPY LEADERSHIP

President Coolidge enjoyed sleeping. Although he started his days early, he also finished them early. Dinner was served at six o'clock, and bedtime came shortly after nine or ten—at the latest. He did not believe in working nights and thought a person who couldn't finish his work in the daytime was not smart. After lunch, Coolidge took a nap each day. Including his nap, he was said to have slept about 11 hours a day. People joked about Coolidge's sleeping habits, and he laughed along with them. One night, he was watching a play when the famous actor Groucho Marx saw him in the audience. From the stage, Marx asked, "Isn't it past your bedtime, Calvin?"

Coolidge's vice president, Charles Dawes, also took regular naps. One time, Dawes's napping got him into trouble. The Senate was deciding whether to approve a man that Coolidge wanted for his **cabinet**. They had reached a tie vote on the issue. Dawes could cast the vote to break the tie in favor of Coolidge's choice. The trouble was, no one could find him. Later, they discovered that Dawes had slipped away to take a nap! Because of this, Coolidge's choice for the cabinet position was not approved.

CHAPTER THREE

STEPPING IN
AS PRESIDENT

arren Harding and Calvin Coolidge were a study in contrasts. Coolidge was small in build and serious. Harding was large and had an easy laugh. Still, the two made a good team and got along well. The contrast between them seemed to appeal to American voters as well. The Harding-Coolidge team had no trouble winning the election of 1920.

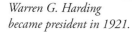

Warren G. Harding became president in 1921.

In his new job as vice president, Coolidge's main duty was to oversee the Senate. He had to keep things running smoothly and stop senators from talking too long. Coolidge rarely interrupted, however. He ran the Senate in his usual calm, silent way. President Harding also allowed him to sit in on cabinet meetings, but Coolidge rarely spoke at them. Another duty he had was to travel across the country to give speeches explaining President Harding's views.

Grace Coolidge was warm and outgoing. A friend once said, "One of Coolidge's greatest assets is Mrs. Coolidge. She will make friends wherever she goes."

He still wasn't comfortable speaking, however. His speeches and answers to questions were usually brief. Soon, Americans were calling him Silent Cal.

Coolidge felt the most uncomfortable at official dinners and social events. At these gatherings, Grace Coolidge produced a warm smile and talked easily with people, while Calvin Coolidge said as little as possible. At a dinner party one evening, the woman sitting next to him said, "You must talk to me, Mr. Coolidge. I

21

wanted to lease it. They offered cabinet member Albert B. Fall $400,000 to lease them the land. Two other members of Harding's cabinet helped Fall make the deal and then cover it up.

Word leaked out about the **bribe,** and the Senate investigated it. Coolidge was an honest man. The scandal made him angry. "Let the guilty be punished," he said. Albert Fall was convicted of bribery and had to pay $100,000. He also spent a year in prison. The other two men resigned in shame. The men involved in the scandal were from the president's own political party and were members of his cabinet. The scandal could have hurt Coolidge's presidency. Instead, the event strengthened his leadership. The American people believed he handled the problem well. They believed he was an honest man.

Secretary of the Interior Albert Fall was at the center of the Teapot Dome scandal. He was convicted of bribery, making him the first cabinet official sent to prison for a crime committed in office.

COOLIDGE'S SMOKE SCREEN

Coolidge enjoyed smoking cigars. At the time, no one knew smoking was dangerous, and many people smoked. Coolidge sometimes smoked three cigars by the afternoon. On summer nights, he would relax in a rocking chair with a cigar while Grace knitted. Coolidge liked high-quality cigars, but because he was frugal, he claimed he rarely bought them. He said that most were gifts. At that time, the cigars he liked cost about 75 cents a piece.

Coolidge used his smoking as a political tool. He often had early breakfasts with lawmakers. They were served the president's favorite meal—pancakes. Then a servant would bring in cigars for everyone. Coolidge used this time to make his case about issues he cared about. Even though it was early in the morning, most lawmakers would light their cigars and smoke them with the president just to keep on his good side.

President Coolidge used his cigar smoking in the same way as he used his silence—to control a conversation or meeting. Instead of answering a question, he might simply take long draws from his cigar and blow out the smoke. This made the other people feel nervous and unsure. He might do this several times until the people he was meeting with either gave up their argument or offered another idea that Coolidge liked better.

Calvin Coolidge's parents raised him to respect all people no matter whether they were rich or poor, black or white. In his First Annual Message to Congress, Coolidge spoke about African Americans, who were at that time often referred to as "colored." "Numbered among our population are 12 million colored people," he pointed out. "Under the Constitution, their rights are just as sacred as those of any other private citizen. It is both a public and private duty to protect those rights." While Coolidge seemed to feel strongly about civil rights, as president he did little to advance the cause of the rights of all people. Yet in conversation, he often made his feelings clear. For example, one day he was walking with Colonel Edmund Starling of the Secret Service when Starling described a man as a "fine colored gentleman." Coolidge did not like this. He corrected Starling by telling him that he should say simply, "a fine gentleman."

THE COUNTRY AND THE KLAN

The Ku Klux Klan was a hate group that started in the southern United States after the Civil War. The Klan hated blacks, Catholics, and Jews. Klansmen wore long robes and masks with pointed hats so that no one would recognize them. Klan members burned crosses to scare people they did not like. They kidnapped some people and beat and killed others. In some cities, the police did nothing about these crimes. Some police shared the Klan's hatred, so they failed to act.

In the 1920s, the Klan grew quickly. By 1924, as many as five million people belonged to the Ku Klux Klan. Some members held political office or were successful businesspeople. The Klan was a major topic during the presidential campaign of 1924.

Some Klan members supported Coolidge's presidential bid. They posted campaign signs on the roadway. They changed the *C's* in his slogan "Keep Cool with Coolidge" to large *K's*. From a distance, only "KKK" was visible. When people asked Coolidge how he felt about the Klan, he did not reply. Finally, an assistant sent out a notice stating that Coolidge was not a member of the Klan and did not have sympathy for them. Reporters argued that Coolidge himself still had not taken a formal stand against the Klan. His assistant then released another statement. It said that those who truly knew Coolidge knew his position on the Klan.

Coolidge never made his feelings about the Klan public. The power of the Klan began to weaken in the years after he won the election. The Klan still exits today, but it has only a few thousand members.

CHAPTER FOUR

THE ROARING TWENTIES

Calvin Coolidge easily won the presidential nomination in 1924. The delegates at the Republican convention selected Charles Dawes to be the vice presidential candidate. Coolidge did not believe it was dignified for the president to campaign for office. Instead, others who supported him campaigned for him. One of their most popular slogans was "Keep Cool with Coolidge."

The **Democrats** had little chance of winning with Coolidge running as the Republican candidate. They had had a difficult time selecting a candidate at their convention. After arguing and voting many times, the Democrats finally chose John W. Davis. But many Democrats did not vote for Davis. Coolidge and Dawes had solid support and easily won the election.

During the campaign, Coolidge had faced a life-changing trauma. His 16-year-old son, Calvin Jr., was

A Coolidge campaign button from 1924

playing a tough tennis match with his brother on the White House lawn when he developed a blister on his foot. The blister grew painful, and a doctor determined that he had blood poisoning. They took Calvin Jr. to the hospital, but the doctors could not cure him. Calvin Jr. died, and his father was devastated. "When he went, the power and glory of the presidency went with him," he remarked. Looking back, many people believed Coolidge never really recovered from this loss. He seemed to lose interest in the business of being president.

Coolidge with vice presidential candidate Charles Dawes. Dawes won the Nobel Peace Prize in 1925 for his efforts to stabilize the German economy in the years after World War I.

29

Coolidge was 52 years old when he was sworn in as president for the second time. In keeping with his values, he did not celebrate his victory with an expensive banquet or a large, elegant ball. He liked to keep things simple and quiet. This was out of step with most Americans during this time. It was the "Roaring Twenties." Many Americans seemed to be enjoying an endless party. Women had more freedom. They had voted in national elections for the first time in 1920 and were moving into the workforce. Many wore short

Fast, high-spirited dances like the Charleston were all the rage in the 1920s.

dresses and the newest bobbed hairstyle. Jazz music became the rage. At parties, people wore themselves out doing a new dance called the Charleston.

People felt happy and confident because of the country's strong **economy.** Though in most businesses, salaries were steady, some people were earning more than they had in the past. At the same time, new inventions—radios, telephones, washing machines, automobiles—were now available. People wanted to buy luxuries they once had only dreamed of owning.

During the 1920s, Americans believed that there was nothing that the United States couldn't do better than the rest of the world. Aviation—the science of flying aircraft—took off. Charles Lindbergh became a national hero when he flew his plane, the *Spirit of St. Louis,* solo across the Atlantic Ocean. The great baseball player Babe Ruth hit a new record of 60 home runs. Americans felt great pride in their country.

Coolidge remained calm during this burst of energy in the country. He did little to change things, and people were happy that he was in the White House. The economy was growing swiftly, and Coolidge encouraged businesses to expand. He helped the economy grow by cutting taxes and paying off some of the national debt, money that the country had borrowed from banks and other sources. In 1925, Coolidge gave a speech to the American Society of Newspaper Editors. He urged the press to keep up with business trends in order to report effectively. "After all," he said, "the chief business of the American people is

Coolidge was the first president to broadcast a presidential address to Congress on the radio. He was also the first to broadcast a speech from the White House. From his office at the White House, his speech on George Washington's birthday went out to 42 stations across the country.

Calvin Coolidge had a mechanical horse installed in the White House. He used it for exercise, but he also enjoyed whooping like cowboys sometimes do when they ride real horses.

In 1924, Coolidge tried to veto an act called the Veteran's Bonus. Congress passed the law despite his efforts. It gave veterans insurance that they could use for up to 20 years.

Coolidge makes a phone call while his wife looks on. Telephones became increasingly common in the 1920s.

business. They are profoundly concerned with buying, selling, investing and prospering in the world." Not everyone was enjoying success at this time, however. Farmers generally did not do well during the 1920s. They had too many crops and nowhere to sell them. Coolidge had grown up on a farm and knew farming was a hard business. Yet twice Coolidge vetoed a bill that would have helped farmers sell crops to other countries. He did this because he thought the government should not interfere in business.

As president, Coolidge worked to keep peace in the world. When **revolutions** broke out in Central America, he sent troops to control them. He sent Ambassador Dwight Morrow to Mexico to stop a war and to protect the right of the United States to mine there. Another Coolidge assistant, Frank Kellogg, went on to work with French leaders on the Kellogg-Briand Pact of 1928. This **treaty** asked nations to stop using war as a way to solve disagreements. Fifteen nations signed the treaty. Although it did not end war in the long run, the treaty was a step in the right direction.

Near the end of his first full term, Coolidge surprised the country with a short announcement. On August 2, 1927, Coolidge said, "I do not choose to run for president in 1928." No one was quite sure why he made this decision. He was a popular president who probably would have easily won another term. Whatever the reason, Coolidge stuck to his word.

After Republican Herbert Hoover became the new president in 1929, Coolidge and his family returned to their house in Northampton. They found that they had little privacy there. Reporters and eager citizens bothered them all the time. Finally, the Coolidges bought a 12-room home nearby called the Beeches. It was surrounded by several acres of land and a gate that gave the family more privacy.

Many American presidents have libraries dedicated solely to their lives and service to the country. Coolidge has no separate library, but a wing in the Forbes Library in Northampton, Massachusetts, is devoted to his life. It is called the Calvin Coolidge Memorial Room. He began donating important documents and photos to the library in 1920 and continued throughout his life.

Grace Coolidge loved animals. She had a number of pets at the White House, including a raccoon named Rebecca.

President Ronald Reagan considered Calvin Coolidge "one of our most underrated presidents." He agreed with many of Coolidge's policies such as tax cuts and smaller government. Reagan hung a portrait of Coolidge in the Cabinet Room of the White House.

Coolidge kept his law office, but he did not practice law. He served on the board of directors for a large company. He also wrote his autobiography, the story of his life. He authored a regular newspaper column called "Thinking Things Over with Calvin Coolidge." But mostly, Coolidge and his wife traveled and lived a quiet life.

In June 1931, Coolidge stopped writing his daily column to spend more time at his family's farm in Plymouth Notch. He told his family and friends that he often felt tired, even doing normal everyday activities. He said that he felt older than he really was. On

January 5, 1933, after a typical morning of checking his mail and working a crossword puzzle, Coolidge went upstairs to shave. Grace Coolidge found the former president on the bathroom floor a short time later. He was dead of a heart attack. Coolidge had died as he had lived—quietly. He was 60 years old.

Thousands of people attended his memorial service. Coolidge was then buried in his family plot in Plymouth Notch, in the Vermont farm country where he had been born and raised. It was a land he had found stirring in its beauty, and it was a land that he loved.

Coolidge working on his farm in Plymouth North, Vermont.

THE BUST AFTER THE BOOM

During Coolidge's time as president, a few people grew very rich. Average people did not, however. Most workers did not see their salaries rise much. Yet during this time, advertisers began tempting the public to buy new gadgets that would make their lives better. Everyone longed for the things that rich people had. To help them buy the things they wanted, businesses began to offer them a new option called credit. Using credit, people could buy something immediately and then pay for it later. People bought many things that they could not afford. They did not save their money as they had in the past.

As the economy grew, the wealthy invested money in the **stock market.** Those with less money also wanted to get rich by investing. Many people had to borrow money to buy stocks. As they invested, the stock market went up. When the stock market went down a little, President Coolidge would assure the people that the economy was still strong. This made the public feel secure, and they invested more money. After a few years, people who had borrowed money for goods or to invest needed to start paying it back. Suddenly, they could no longer buy new things. Many could not even pay their bills.

And then, just seven months after Coolidge left Washington, the stock market crashed. Many people lost money that day. The United States fell into the worst economic period in its history, called the Great **Depression.** Millions of businesspeople lost all their money and had to shut down their companies. Workers couldn't find jobs, and people were left homeless and hungry. In the early 1930s, when the Depression was at its worst, 15 million Americans were out of work. Many had no money and relied on soup kitchens to get food.

Some historians think that Coolidge saw the Depression coming. They believe that was why he did not seek another term as president. Perhaps he did not want to take the blame for the upcoming bad times.

After he retired, Coolidge said about the Depression: "There has been a general lack of judgment so widespread as to involve practically the whole country. We have learned that we were not so big as we thought we were. We shall have to keep nearer to the ground. We shall not feel so elated, but we shall be much safer."

1870	1880	1890	1900	1910

1872
Calvin Coolidge is born on July 4 in Plymouth Notch, Vermont. His parents are John and Victoria Coolidge.

1884
Victoria Coolidge dies after being thrown from a runaway horse.

1890
Calvin's sister, Abigail Coolidge, becomes ill with appendicitis. Calvin stays by her side until she dies. Coolidge graduates from the Black River Academy in Ludlow, Vermont.

1895
Coolidge graduates from Amherst College with honors. He begins working as an assistant at a law firm in Northampton, Massachusetts.

1897
Calvin Coolidge passes an exam that allows him to practice law in Massachusetts. He opens his first law office. He also begins to work for the Republican Party.

1898
Coolidge is elected a city councilman in Northampton, Massachusetts.

1900
Coolidge is elected city attorney of Northampton.

1905
On October 4, Coolidge marries Grace Anna Goodhue.

1906
Coolidge is elected to the Massachusetts House of Representatives.

1909
Coolidge is elected mayor of Northampton.

1912
Coolidge becomes a member of the Massachusetts Senate.

1914
Coolidge serves as president of the Massachusetts Senate.

1915
Coolidge is elected lieutenant governor of Massachusetts.

1919
Coolidge becomes the governor of Massachusetts. The Boston police go on strike, leaving the city unprotected. Violence breaks out, and Coolidge calls in the National Guard to take control of the city. He supports the police commissioner's decision to fire the striking police. President Woodrow Wilson writes to Coolidge to praise him for his actions.

1920

The Republican Party chooses Warren G. Harding as its presidential candidate. Coolidge is chosen as the vice presidential candidate. Harding and Coolidge win the election.

1923

On August 2, Harding dies suddenly in San Francisco. Early the next morning, Coolidge is sworn in as president of the United States in his father's home in Plymouth Notch, Vermont. The Teapot Dome scandal surfaces, and the American people learn of illegal activities in Harding's cabinet.

1924

Calvin Coolidge Jr. dies from blood poisoning after getting a blister while playing tennis on the White House lawn. On November 4, Calvin Coolidge is elected president. Charles Dawes is elected vice president.

1927

Charles Lindbergh makes his historic flight across the Atlantic Ocean. Baseball great Babe Ruth hits a record 60 home runs in one season. Coolidge surprises the nation by announcing he will not seek another term as president.

1928

The Kellogg-Briand Pact is written and signed by 15 nations. This agreement is designed to help nations find new ways to settle their differences instead of going to war.

1929

Herbert Hoover becomes the nation's 31st president. Coolidge returns to Northampton, where he leads a quiet life. He writes his autobiography and a daily newspaper column. In October, the stock market crashes, and the Great Depression begins. By the early 1930s, 15 million Americans are out of work.

1933

On January 5, Calvin Coolidge dies suddenly from a heart attack. He is buried in Plymouth Notch, Vermont.

OUR PRESIDENT
DEEDS - NOT WORDS

GLOSSARY

bill (BILL) A bill is an idea for a new law that is presented to a group of lawmakers. Coolidge signed a bill that limited the workweek for women and children to 40 hours.

bribe (BRYB) A bribe is a reward (such as money) that is offered in an attempt to get a person to do something wrong. The Teapot Dome scandal started when oil companies offered a bribe to a member of President Harding's cabinet.

cabinet (KAB-nit) A cabinet is the group of people who advise a president. President Harding allowed Coolidge to sit in on cabinet meetings.

campaign (kam-PAYN) A campaign is the process of running for an election, including activities such as giving speeches or attending rallies. Coolidge campaigned for the position of governor of Massachusetts.

candidate (KAN-duh-date) A candidate is a person running in an election. Coolidge was a candidate for many political offices.

delegates (DE-li-gutz) Delegates are people elected to take part in something. Delegates at the 1920 Republican convention chose Warren G. Harding as their candidate for president.

Democrats (DEM-uh-krats) Democrats are people who belong to the Democratic Party, one of the two major political parties in the United States. Coolidge defeated the Democratic candidate in 1924.

depression (dih-PRE-shun) A depression is a period of time in which there is little business activity and many people are out of work. The Great Depression began in 1929.

economy (ee-KON-uh-mee) An economy is the way money is earned and spent. The nation had a strong economy while Coolidge was president.

militia (muh-LISH-uh) A militia is a volunteer army made up of citizens who have trained as soldiers. The mayor of Boston called in the state militia during the 1919 Boston police strike.

nomination (nom-ih-NAY-shun) If someone receives a nomination, he or she is chosen to run for an office, such as the presidency. Calvin Coolidge received a surprise nomination as the Republican candidate for vice president in 1920.

notary public (NOH-tuh-ree PUB-lik) A notary public is a person who certifies that documents are legal. As a notary public, John Coolidge was able to swear in Calvin Coolidge as president.

political parties (puh-LIT-uh-kul PAR-teez) Political parties are groups of people who share similar ideas about how to run a government. The Republican Party is one of the nation's two major political parties.

Prohibition (pro-uh-BI-shun) Prohibition was a law banning the manufacture or the sale of alcohol. Prohibition went into effect in 1920.

repealed (ri-PEELD) A law is repealed if government leaders vote to end it. Prohibition was repealed in 1933.

Republican Party (re-PUB-lih-ken PAR-tee) The Republican Party is one of the two major political parties in the United States. Coolidge was a member of the Republican Party.

revolutions (rev-uh-LOO-shunz) Revolutions are protests and warfare intended to cause a change in government. When revolutions broke out in Central America, Coolidge sent troops to help.

scandal (SKAN-dl) A scandal is a shameful action that shocks the public. After President Harding died, the country learned about the Teapot Dome scandal.

stock market (STAWK MAR-kit) The stock market is where people buy and sell pieces of ownership in different companies, called shares or stock. Companies share their profits with people who own their stock.

term (TERM) A term of office is the length of time politicians can keep their positions by law before another election is held. The president's term is four years.

treaty (TREE-tee) A treaty is a formal agreement between nations. The Kellogg-Briand Pact was a treaty that asked nations to stop using war as a way to solve disagreements.

veterans (VET-er-enz) Veterans are people who served in the military, especially during a war. Coolidge worked to help veterans of World War I find decent places to live.

vetoed (VEE-tohd) A bill is vetoed if a president or governor rejects it. As governor, Coolidge vetoed a bill allowing the sale of beer or wine.

THE UNITED STATES GOVERNMENT

The United States government is divided into three equal branches: the executive, the legislative, and the judicial. This division helps prevent abuses of power because each branch has to answer to the other two. No one branch can become too powerful.

EXECUTIVE BRANCH

PRESIDENT
VICE PRESIDENT
DEPARTMENTS

The job of the executive branch is to enforce the laws. It is headed by the president, who serves as the spokesperson for the United States around the world. The president signs bills into law and appoints important officials such as federal judges. He or she is also the commander in chief of the U.S. military. The president is assisted by the vice president, who takes over if the president dies or cannot carry out the duties of the office.

The executive branch also includes various departments, each focused on a specific topic. They include the Defense Department, the Justice Department, and the Agriculture Department. The department heads, along with other officials such as the vice president, serve as the president's closest advisers, called the cabinet.

LEGISLATIVE BRANCH

CONGRESS
Senate and
House of Representatives

The job of the legislative branch is to make the laws. It consists of Congress, which is divided into two parts: the Senate and the House of Representatives. The Senate has 100 members, and the House of Representatives has 435 members. Each state has two senators. The number of representatives a state has varies depending on the state's population.

Besides making laws, Congress also passes budgets and enacts taxes. In addition, it is responsible for declaring war, maintaining the military, and regulating trade with other countries.

JUDICIAL BRANCH

SUPREME COURT
COURTS OF APPEALS
DISTRICT COURTS

The job of the judicial branch is to interpret the laws. It consists of the nation's federal courts. Trials are held in district courts. During trials, judges must decide what laws mean and how they apply. Courts of appeals review the decisions made in district courts.

The nation's highest court is the Supreme Court. If someone disagrees with a court of appeals ruling, he or she can ask the Supreme Court to review it. The Supreme Court may refuse. The Supreme Court makes sure that decisions and laws do not violate the Constitution.

CHOOSING
THE PRESIDENT

It may seem odd, but American voters don't elect the president directly. Instead, the president is chosen using what is called the Electoral College.

Each state gets as many votes in the Electoral College as its combined total of senators and representatives in Congress. For example, Iowa has two senators and five representatives, so it gets seven electoral votes. Although the District of Columbia does not have any voting members in Congress, it gets three electoral votes. Usually, the candidate who wins the most votes in any given state receives all of that state's electoral votes.

To become president, a candidate must get more than half of the Electoral College votes. There are a total of 538 votes in the Electoral College, so a candidate needs 270 votes to win. If nobody receives 270 Electoral College votes, the House of Representatives chooses the president.

With the Electoral College system, the person who receives the most votes nationwide does not always receive the most electoral votes. This happened most recently in 2000, when Al Gore received half a million more national votes than George W. Bush. Bush became president because he had more Electoral College votes.

THE WHITE HOUSE

The White House is the official home of the president of the United States. It is located at 1600 Pennsylvania Avenue NW in Washington, D.C. In 1792, a contest was held to select the architect who would design the president's home. James Hoban won. Construction took eight years.

The first president, George Washington, never lived in the White House. The second president, John Adams, moved into the house in 1800, though the inside was not yet complete. During the War of 1812, British soldiers burned down much of the White House. It was rebuilt several years later.

The White House was changed through the years. Porches were added, and President Theodore Roosevelt added the West Wing. President William Taft changed the shape of the presidential office, making it into the famous Oval Office. While Harry Truman was president, the old house was discovered to be structurally weak. All the walls were reinforced with steel, and the rooms were rebuilt.

Today, the White House has 132 rooms (including 35 bathrooms), 28 fireplaces, and 3 elevators. It takes 570 gallons of paint to cover the outside of the six-story building. The White House provides the president with many ways to relax. It includes a putting green, a jogging track, a swimming pool, a tennis court, and beautifully landscaped gardens. The White House also has a movie theater, a billiard room, and a one-lane bowling alley.

PRESIDENTIAL PERKS

The job of president of the United States is challenging. It is probably one of the most stressful jobs in the world. Because of this, presidents are paid well, though not nearly as well as the leaders of large corporations. In 2007, the president earned $400,000 a year. Presidents also receive extra benefits that make the demanding job a little more appealing.

★ **Camp David:** In the 1940s, President Franklin D. Roosevelt chose this heavily wooded spot in the mountains of Maryland to be the presidential retreat, where presidents can relax. Even though it is a retreat, world business is conducted there. Most famously, President Jimmy Carter met with Middle Eastern leaders at Camp David in 1978. The result was a peace agreement between Israel and Egypt.

★ *Air Force One:* The president flies on a jet called *Air Force One.* It is a Boeing 747-200B that has been modified to meet the president's needs.

Air Force One is the size of a large home. It is equipped with a dining room, sleeping quarters, a conference room, and office space. It also has two kitchens that can provide food for up to 50 people.

★ **The Secret Service:** While not the most glamorous of the president's perks, the Secret Service is one of the most important. The Secret Service is a group of highly trained agents who protect the president and the president's family.

★ **The Presidential State Car:** The presidential limousine is a stretch Cadillac DTS.

It has been armored to protect the president in case of attack. Inside the plush car are a foldaway desk, an entertainment center, and a communications console.

★ **The Food:** The White House has five chefs who will make any food the president wants. The White House also has an extensive wine collection.

★ **Retirement:** A former president receives a pension, or retirement pay, of just under $180,000 a year. Former presidents also receive Secret Service protection for the rest of their lives.

F A C T S

QUALIFICATIONS

To run for president, a candidate must

- ★ be at least 35 years old
- ★ be a citizen who was born in the United States
- ★ have lived in the United States for 14 years

TERM OF OFFICE

A president's term of office is four years.
No president can stay in office for more than two terms.

ELECTION DATE

The presidential election takes place every four years on the first Tuesday of November.

INAUGURATION DATE

Presidents are inaugurated on January 20.

OATH OF OFFICE

I do solemnly swear I will faithfully execute the office of the President of the United States and will to the best of my ability preserve, protect, and defend the Constitution of the United States.

WRITE A LETTER TO THE PRESIDENT

One of the best things about being a U.S. citizen is that Americans get to participate in their government. They can speak out if they feel government leaders aren't doing their jobs. They can also praise leaders who are going the extra mile. Do you have something you'd like the president to do? Should the president worry more about the environment and encourage people to recycle? Should the government spend more money on our schools? You can write a letter to the president to say how you feel!

1600 Pennsylvania Avenue
Washington, D.C. 20500
You can even send an e-mail to: president@whitehouse.gov

BOOKS

Feinstein, Stephen. *The 1920s from Prohibition to Charles Lindbergh*. Berkeley Heights, NJ: Enslow Publishers, 2006.

Feldmean, Ruth Tenzer. *Calvin Coolidge*. Minneapolis: Lerner Publishing Group, 2005.

Freedman, Russell. *Children of the Great Depression*. New York: Clarion Books, 2005.

Gow, Mary. *The Stock Market Crash of 1929: Dawn of the Great Depression*. Berkeley Heights, NJ: Enslow Publishers, 2003.

Howes, Kelly King and Carnagie, Julie. *Roaring Twenties: Almanac and Primary Sources Edition 1*. Farmington Hills, MI: Gale Group, 2005.

Vecchione, Glen. *The Little Giant Book of American Presidents*. New York: Sterling, 2007.

VIDEOS

The American President. DVD (Hollywood, CA: PBS Paramount, 2000).

The History Channel Presents The Presidents. DVD (New York: A&E Home Video, 2005).

National Geographic's Inside the White House. DVD (Washington, DC: National Geographic Video, 2003).

INTERNET SITES

Visit our Web page for lots of links about Calvin Coolidge and other U.S. presidents:

http://www.childsworld.com/links

Note to Parents, Teachers, and Librarians: We routinely verify our Web links to make sure they are safe, active sites—so encourage your readers to check them out!

INDEX